SPANDEX HABITS

S-T-R-E-T-C-H YOUR ROUTINES TO FIT INTO YOUR LIFE

Custom Habit Planner Included

MICHELLE KULP

Copyright © 2020 Michelle Kulp

Published by: Monarch Crown Publishing

All Rights Reserved. No part of this book may be reproduced in any form without permission in writing from the author. Reviewers may quote brief passages in reviews.

ISBN: 978-1-7354188-1-0

Table of Contents

Introduction 1

Chapter 1 – Clarity Questions 7

Chapter 2 – Outsmarting Motivation 31

Chapter 3 – Pesky Procrastination 39

Chapter 4 – Marginal Gains 49

Chapter 5 – The Building Blocks of *Spandex Habits* 55

Chapter 6 – Habit Stacking 65

Chapter 7 – Reverse Engineering Bad Habits 73

Chapter 8 – Spandex Habits – Custom Planner 83

Closing Thoughts 93

Can You Do Me A Favor? 95

"Be not afraid of going slowly, be afraid only of standing still."
~ *Chinese Proverb*

"A habit is something you do without thinking."
~ *Jeff Olson, author of The Slight Edge*

"Do the thing and you shall have the power."
~ *Ralph Waldo Emerson*

"Your life does not get better by chance, it gets better by *change*."
~ *Jim Rohn*

"You've got to get up every morning with determination if you're going to go to bed with satisfaction.
~ *George Lorimer*

"An extraordinary life is all about daily, continuous improvements in the areas that matter most.
~ *Robin Sharma*

"Discipline creates lifestyle."
~ *Peter Voogd*

"Everything is difficult before it's easy."
~ *Hal Elrod, Miracle Morning*

" Success is the timely pursuit of your intentions."
~ *Clarry Lay*

Introduction

You've probably heard this quote by Benjamin Disraeli:

"Change is inevitable. Change is constant."

If I asked you how your life has changed in the past 6-12 months, you could probably list dozens of ways – desired or not.

In the past few years, the following events occurred in my life:

- My mother passed away from breast cancer

- My youngest daughter gave birth to my first grand-daughter

- My daughter and grand-daughter came to live with me temporarily (it's been a year now), which means I get a lot more babysitting time

- I moved to a new house

- My son and his wife recently gave birth to my second beautiful granddaughter

- The COVID-19 pandemic changed many aspects of my life

- My business has increased three-fold

- I ended a four-year on-again, off-again relationship

- I fractured my foot in three places

- My personal assistant who I relied on heavily moved to another state

- My virtual assistant who had worked with me for five years left to work exclusively with one client

- I made a commitment to write and publish a book a month

When life changes from day to day, the question is...

How do we stick with our habits or create new habits to achieve ALL our dreams and goals amid a constantly evolving, stressful, and chaotic life?

Unfortunately, many of us are unrealistic about our goals because we often imagine an ideal situation, where there are no limitations on our time or energy levels.

We love setting BIG lofty goals, but when life happens, and we can't follow through with those, our response is usually to do NOTHING.

Enter Spandex Habits – a system that will help you bend your goals to whatever works best for you, on any given day, without abandoning your habits altogether.

Just like clothing made with *spandex*, **Spandex Habits** are stretchy and adaptable for you.

I don't know about you, but the older I get, the more I love Spandex in my clothing. I start to feel restricted and constrained when I wear clothes that don't have a little bit of that magical stretchiness. As my body changes (a few pounds up or a few pounds down), Spandex clothing changes with me, and I love it.

Did you know that Spandex can stretch to over 500% of its original size?

Spandex saves me money because I don't need to buy new clothes when I gain or lose a little weight; as long as I have a little Spandex, I'm good.

Don't our habits and goals deserve that extra "give" and "flexibility" so they change with us and for us?

Spandex is an anagram for "E X P A N D S."

You can EXPAND your life by prioritizing yourself and creating flexible *Spandex Habits* that support your goals.

This book is not about one-size-fits-all habits as those don't work. When our lives change (as they always do), we can't fit those one-size-fits-all habits into our lives; so we often abandon those habits.

Spandex Habits will transform an existing habit (once we clarify our goals) into three sizes:

1. Mini
2. Maxi
3. Massive

Think of ***Spandex Habits*** in terms of Starbucks drink sizes (my daughter loves this analogy):

1. Tall
2. Grande
3. Venti

Any habit can be "**Minified**" and still have a big impact if done consistently over a period of time. ***Spandex Habits***, including mini habits, will move you significantly closer to your goals in a smart and strategic way.

You can also add variety to your habit repertoire so you don't get bored using the same method to achieve your goals.

I use *Spandex Habits* every day. One of my goals is to be fit and exercise every day to offset the extensive amount of time I sit at my computer, running my online business and writing books. Using *Spandex Habits*, I now have multiple habit "choices" that help me get fit (walking, yoga, going to the gym, riding my bike) and choices on how to get them done (mini, maxi, and massive).

I also use *Spandex Habits* for writing. Since January of 2020, I have been writing a book a month. At first, it was hard to get on a consistent writing schedule, but once I implemented *Spandex Habits*, it became so much easier. This year, I have written, published, and launched seven books. You are reading the eighth book.

How did I do it?

Instead of having a one-size-fits-all goal (like many authors do) such as writing ten pages per day or 5,000 words per day, I created a flexible writing plan for myself:

- **Mini** – I write two pages for my book per day

- **Maxi** – I write one chapter for my book per day

- **Massive** – I write two chapters for my book per day

I write short books (100-125 pages), so a chapter might be 5-10 pages. I've been able to achieve all of my writing goals using *Spandex Habits*.

Compare this to 2019 (pre-*Spandex Habits*); it took me an entire year to write the second edition of my book, *Quit Your Job and Follow Your Dreams*.

Without *Spandex Habits*, you wouldn't be reading this book.

When you create ***Spandex Habits,*** you should include variety in your activities. To publish a book a month, I don't have to *write* each day. I can choose other tasks that move me closer to completing my goal like editing, proofing, outlining, cover design, etc.

***Spandex Habits* allows you to create more FREEDOM in your life while you achieve remarkable results.**

For example, I walk every day but didn't have a lot of time today because I was taking care of my three-year-old granddaughter. So, I utilized my "Spandex *Mini* Habit," which was a ½-mile walk around the neighborhood (my *Maxi* habit is a 1½-mile a mile walk, and my *Massive* habit is a 3-mile walk.) Having these three options gives me a WIN no matter which level I choose, and I feel good about myself, knowing I am achieving my fitness goals.

Consistency is the KEY, and we'll learn more about that in the Marginal Gains chapter.

I can't wait to help you create your ***Flexible Habit Plan*** to start achieving your dreams and goals.

This book contains three sections:

1. Clarity, Motivation, and Procrastination
2. Marginal Gains, the Building Blocks of *Spandex Habits,* and Habit Stacking
3. Reverse Engineering Bad Habits and Your Custom Spandex Habits Planner

You can implement ***Spandex Habits*** in all areas of your life—personal, family, business, career, finances, and more.

If you're ready to start creating ***Flexible Habits*** that work for you as your life continually evolves, changes, and grows, let's get started!

Circular Habit Tracker

NOTE: I believe in the power of writing things down and creating a visual way to track your new *Spandex Habits*. To do this, we'll be using this Etsy template Habit Tracker, which will make tracking your daily habits fun, visual, and easy.

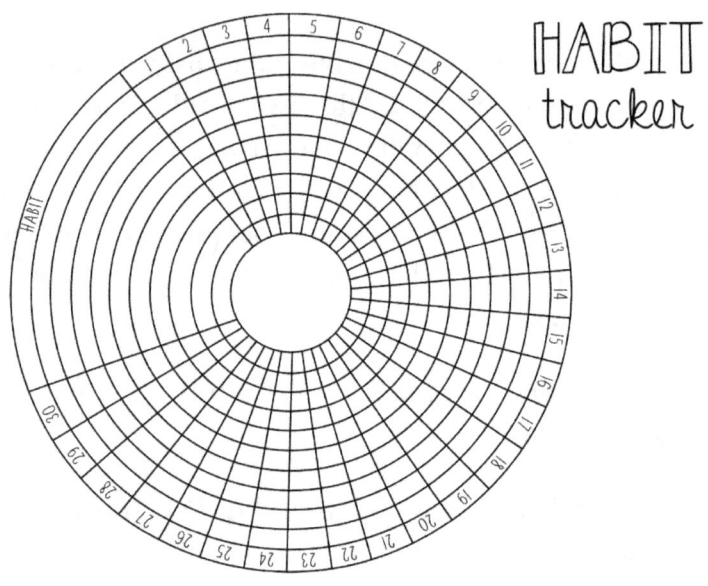

Chapter 1 – Clarity Questions

Ambiguous goals are hard to achieve because they are elusive and antithetical to making progress.

So, before we talk about habits, we must be specific about what we want to achieve. There are two types of goals – **Broad** (vague) and **Behavioral** (action-based). Broad goals include statements like 'I want to be more organized.'

A behavioral goal has three elements:

1. Can be broken down into specific steps

2. Includes action steps

3. You will know when you have achieved it

So, "I want to be more organized" becomes "I will declutter and organize my bedroom, closet, and bathroom before September 1st."

Unfortunately, most of us don't include this level of clarity with our goals that would enable us to map out specific steps to achieve them.

We can't measure results for goals like "I want more money, a better body, a nice place to live, to get out of debt, a loving partner, etc." because they are vague, and we cannot determine when we achieve the goal.

So, how do we figure out what we want and get that added clarity?

By asking the right questions.

Einstein once said,

"If I had an hour to solve a problem and my life depended on the solution, I would spend the first 55 minutes determining the proper question to ask; for once I know the proper question, I could solve the problem in less than five minutes."

Einstein was a brilliant man.

In his #1 Wall Street Journal bestselling book, *The One Thing*, Gary Keller, founder of Keller Williams Realty, Inc., wrote:

"Life is a question. You may be asking, 'Why focus on a question when what we really crave is an answer?' It's simple. Answers come from questions, and the quality of any answer is directly determined by the quality of the question. Ask the wrong question, get the wrong answer. Ask the right question, get the right answer. Ask the most powerful question possible, and the answer can be life altering."

Over the years, I, too, have learned the power of asking the right questions.

I wrote an entire book about questions in my #1 bestseller, *How to Find Your Passion: 23 Questions that Can Change Your Entire Life*. We're going to use a few questions from that book here as well as some new ones.

WRITE IT DOWN

Dr. Gail Matthews, a psychology professor at the Dominican University in California, led a study on goal-setting with over 250 participants and found that you are 42 percent more likely to achieve your goals if you write them down.

Writing down our goals forces us to get clear about what we want to accomplish and create ways to achieve our desired results.

Grant Cardone, self-made millionaire and bestselling author of many books including *The 10X Rule,* writes his goals twice a day – once in the morning and again in the evening. This ensures he doesn't have amnesia about his goals.

Writing down your goals is imperative to your success!

Invest in a journal or notebook for these exercises and record your thoughts on paper or just write in this book. Whatever you do, don't rely on your memory, because in a few days you'll forget everything you were *thinking*.

Doing this will help you access your right brain – the creative brain – instead of "thinking" only with your "logical" left-brain. You need to listen to your heart and soul and not only your logical mind.

NOTE: The following are timed writing exercises. Set the timer on your phone for three minutes per question and write as fast as you can without lifting your pen from the paper; this will ensure you access your creative brain.

CLARITY QUESTIONS

What do I hate in my life right now?

_____
_____
_____
_____
_____
_____
_____
_____
_____
_____
_____
_____
_____
_____
_____

For each item listed above, write the opposite. For example, if you wrote, "I hate waking up early for work," the opposite might be, "I love sleeping until 9 a.m. and working on my own schedule."

What do I truly want, but don't believe I can have?

What do I want to eliminate or have less of in my life?

What makes me so heated and angry I can't stand it?

If I had a magic wand, I would change these three things in my life right now.

What have I been struggling with for months or years?

How is my life out of balance?

What are three ways I create obstacles in my life, and why do I do that?

What has my inner voice been saying to me that I have been ignoring?

In what ways am I "waiting" to start living?

What gives me energy, and what depletes my energy?

What am I procrastinating about right now, and why?

Great job! The key is to be honest when answering. Once we have more clarity, we can create our goals based on that clarity.

Universally, we all want similar things such as:

- Happiness

- To be loved

- Financial freedom

- Great friends and family

- A safe and beautiful home

- Good health

- Living a good life

- Time freedom

- People that inspire us

- A safe mode of transportation

- Respect

It's easy to mistake these "universal goals" for our life plans. Unfortunately, these goals don't equate to having a *plan*, because they are too vague, don't include specific steps, can't be measured, and don't have a completion date. They sound good, but we can't break them down into specific, actionable steps.

If you are unsure what your goals are, I have some tools you can use to determine them.

Introducing…

THE PASSION TEST

Janet Bray Attwood and Chris Attwood, co-authors of *The Passion Test: The Effortless Path to Discovering Your Destiny,* say that our passions are "the most important things you can think of which would give you a life of joy, passion, and fulfillment."

Janet and Chris created the Passion Test®, a two-part test that helps people discover their purpose and destiny.

It's important to clarify your passions so you can align your goals with them and begin to create and design a life you truly love.

Passion Test – Part One

List your top 10-12 passions/goals/dreams/desires (the most important things you can think of that would give you a life of joy, passion, and fulfillment) by completing the following sentence:

"When my life is ideal, I am:

_____."

Begin each passion statement with a verb, such as being, doing or having. Close your eyes and picture your ideal life and then write your list.

Below are some examples:

When my life is ideal…

- I am at my perfect weight and have lots of energy.
- I am working 20 hours per week and making six figures.

- I am running a marathon twice a year.
- I am married to my dream partner.
- I am running my own online business.
- I am debt-free.
- I am giving back through my non-profit organization.
- I am teaching cooking classes for vegans.
- I am travelling the world first class.
- I am working with an enlightened team.
- I am making a difference in the lives of others.
- I am speaking to large groups of people.
- I am a multi-millionaire.
- I am a bestselling author.
- I am being of service to thousands of people.
- I am having fun.
- I am helping others create and live their vision.
- I am working for myself in my own business.
- I am living in a beautiful home on the water.
- I am hosting writer's retreats twice a year.
- I am teaching online programs that help others.
- I am painting in my studio every day.
- I am hiking in nature.

NOTE: You don't need to include details of how you will make this happen; it's just about the feeling of joy and fulfillment when you are doing these things.

Okay, now it's your turn…

When my life is ideal, I am… (Write the first 10-12 things that come to your mind as fast as you can).

_____
_____
_____
_____
_____
_____
_____
_____
_____
_____
_____
_____
_____

Passion Test – Part Two

Once you've written your passions, select the top three that are most important to you.

Start with #1 and #2. Which one is more important? If #2 is more important, then, compare #2 to #3 and decide which one of those is more important and compare that one to #4. Go through the entire list to get your top three choices.

Magic happens when we get clarity in our lives. It's easy to say, "I hate my job…" but when you ask someone specifically what else they want to do, most people don't have an answer. After doing these exercises, you will know what is important to you, and you can start setting goals based on your passion list.

Repeat this exercise every six months since you are continually evolving and growing. You may have already achieved what was important six months ago, or it's no longer as important to you, and something new might take its place.

Also, once you have your **Spandex Habits** in place and they are running on autopilot, then you can enhance it with "habit stacking" (small routines) to get more bang for your buck.

List your top three passions/goals/dreams from the exercise above:

1. _____

2. _____

3. _____

Now, let's transform your vague answers into more specific goals.

For example, let's say you wrote, "My life is ideal when I am at my perfect weight."

Let's turn that into: "My life is ideal when I am at my perfect weight of 140 pounds with a BMI of 20 by December 25th."

"I am debt free" becomes "I will pay off **[number of cards]** credit cards **[list specific cards and balances]** by this date: _____. I plan to pay off **[Card 1]** first, **[Card 2]** next, and **[Card 3]** last."

Pick 3

Let's limit the number of goals to three for now because most people don't follow through with their goals if they become overwhelmed.

Control Group Study

What do you need to ensure you are successful with your goals?

About twenty years ago, researchers in Great Britain conducted a study to help build better exercise habits in two weeks. To do this, they divided 248 participants into three groups:

1. Control Group
2. Motivation Group with reading materials
3. Motivation Group with plans

The Control Group was asked to track how often they exercised and weren't given any further instructions.

The Motivation Group (with reading materials) was also asked to track how often they exercised and were provided with reading materials on the benefits of exercise.

The Motivation Group (with plans) were asked to do the same as the Motivation Group with reading materials. They were also asked to formulate a plan for WHEN and WHERE they would exercise using the following template:

"During the next week, I will partake in at least 20 minutes of vigorous exercise on **[DAY]** at **[TIME]** in **[PLACE]**.

Results

- 35-38% of the members of the Control Group and Motivation Group with reading materials began exercising.

- The Motivation Group with plans had 91% success rate – more than double the rate of the other two groups!

Having details and an "**INTENTION PLAN**" is the key to being successful.

Can you see the difference between when you have NO details or plans and when you include more specific information?

List the top three goals you want to focus on with specifics (dates, times, amounts, weight, BMI, geography, people, timelines, etc.)

1. _____

2. _____

3. _____

Congratulations for taking the time to get more clarity in your life!

When you create your custom *Spandex Habits Plan,* you'll have several ways to achieve your goals within different time frames. We'll talk more about this in the chapter on how *Spandex Habits* work.

In the next chapter, we will talk about motivation since it's one of the biggest excuses people use for NOT following through with their habits/goals. At one time or another, we've all said, "I'm not motivated today" or "I just don't feel like it."

Chapter 2 – Outsmarting Motivation

To better understand motivation, let's talk about killer whales.

In his bestselling book, *Whale Done! The Power of Positive Relationships,* Ken Blanchard explains how they train 5,000 and 10,000-pound killer whales at Sea World.

First, they establish trust with the whale so the whale knows the trainers won't harm them. Once trust is established, which can take a long time, they begin training.

Blanchard talks about the ABC's of Performance:

A – **Activator** (Action or event that gets the performance going)

B – **Behavior** (The performance that occurs)

C – **Consequence** (The response to the performance)

Ken Blanchard and his team use these ABC's of performance in their business coaching programs.

Here's how it works:

"Let's start with the A, the Activator... The trainers at Sea World use signals to cue what they want the animal to do – arm or hand signals, slapping the water, or tooting a whistle. With people, an Activator can be a set of instructions, a training experience... The most common Activators are goals. **All good performance starts with clear goals**. After you motivate the performance you want by setting clear goals, you have to observe the behavior that follows. That's what B stands for. With a killer whale, that behavior might be jumping into the air, giving a trainer a ride around the pool, splashing the audience with his tail or taking a bow…the most important step in managing performance: the C or Consequence – what happens after you get the behavior you were looking for…When a good performance is followed by something positive, naturally people want to continue that behavior."

The Science of How Habits Work

In his book, *The Power of Habit,* Charles Duhigg explains a 3-step process for creating habits:

1. Cue

2. Routine (that comes from a craving)

3. Reward

"Over time, this loop – Cue, Routine, Reward – becomes more automatic. The cue and reward become intertwined until a powerful sense of ***anticipation*** and ***craving*** emerges."

This is how habits are born. The great news is we don't have to wait to feel "motivated," which may or may not ever happen.

However, we do need to have strong ***cravings*** to be successful with our habits.

Let's dig into this a little deeper.

The Cue triggers your brain to initiate a behavior and predicts a reward. Cues are meaningless unless they are interpreted.

Cravings are the "motivational" force behind the behavior/routine because we have no reason to act without some level of desire to change.

In his book, *Atomic Habits*, James Clear states, "What you crave is not the habit itself but the change in state it delivers."

This is a very important distinction.

For example, you don't want to turn the television on, you want to be entertained. James Clear goes on to say, "Every craving is linked to a desire to change your internal state. Cravings differ from person to person."

The routine/response/behavior is the actual habit you perform; whether a response occurs depends on how intense your craving is.

Last, is the reward.

Rewards are the end goal for creating habits because they satisfy our cravings and teach us that actions are worth remembering. Our brain is a reward detector in many ways, always looking to make that connection.

Clear says, "If a behavior is insufficient in any of the four stages, it will not become a habit. Eliminate the cue and your habit will never start. Reduce the craving and you won't experience enough motivation to act. Make the behavior difficult and you won't be able to do it. And if the reward fails to satisfy your desire, then you'll have no reason to do it again in the future."

Clear's system for creating good habits and eliminating bad habits is outlined below:

How to *Create a Good Habit*

1. Cue – Make it obvious

2. Craving – Make it attractive

3. Response – Make it easy

4. Reward – Make it satisfying

How to *Break a Bad Habit*

1. Cue – Make it invisible

2. Craving – Make it unattractive

3. Response – Make it difficult

4. Reward – Make it unsatisfying

Differences Between Duhigg's 3-Step Method and Clear's 4-Step Method

Charles Duhigg includes only three steps because he believes that our *cravings* come from our behaviors and responses. James Clear includes *cravings* as a fourth step. Either way, our *cravings* must be substantial enough to motivate and prompt us to want to perform the behavior.

So if you find yourself lacking motivation, you now know where to look– **Cue, Craving, Behavior, Reward.** When you are not motivated, something is lacking in one of these four areas. Often, we are not "craving" the reward enough to prompt us to take action.

Charles Duhigg on Different Cravings for Different People Who Exercise:

"In one group, 92 percent of people said they habitually exercised because it made them feel good – they grew to expect and *crave* the endorphins and other neurochemicals a workout provided. In another group, 67 percent of people said that working out gave them a sense of accomplishment – they had come to *crave* a regular sense of triumph from tracking their performance and that self-reward was enough to make the physical activity into a habit."

Think about a few of the good or bad habits you currently have and try to identify your *Craving*:

HABIT #1:
___

HABIT #2:
___

HABIT #3:
___

My Habits

Habit #1: Exercise – I crave the endorphins, how much better I feel mentally, and the energy "high" I get.

Habit #2: No sugar, no flour food lifestyle – I *crave* the increased energy I have when I avoid these foods.

Habit #3: Vegan eating – I am motivated by staying away from doctors and hospitals. This is a different kind of *craving* (avoidance), but it is still a *craving*. The craving is something I *don't* want, but it's still a powerful motivator for me.

If you have a bad habit of smoking, you are probably craving the nicotine, and your cue might be drinking coffee, eating a good meal, or simply seeing a pack of cigarettes. The reward might be that it relieves your anxiety.

When you have a bad habit you want to break, it's important to look at the cues, cravings, behavior, and rewards so you can adjust those accordingly.

Cravings Are Critical

Duhigg says "Cravings are what drive habits. And figuring out how to spark a craving makes creating a new habit easier."

Let's examine one of the goals you wrote down in Chapter 1 to come up with your own steps for creating habits.

Remember, when you have established habits and routines, you don't need motivation.

Goal:

1. **Cue**:
   _____

2. **Craving**:
   _____

3. **Routine/Behavior**:
   _____

4. **Reward**:
   _____

Here's my 4-step plan for doing yoga regularly:

Goal: Do Yoga (at least 3 times per week) for greater flexibility.

1. **Cue**: Yoga mat and clothes next to my bed so I see them first thing in the morning.

2. **Craving**: Feeling flexible and agile without constant neck and back pain.

3. **Routine/Behavior**: 20-minute Yoga CD routine.

4. **Reward**: A sense of accomplishment by writing on my Habits Tracker that I completed my yoga routine. Occasionally, I will buy a new yoga outfit.

Of course, the reward could be anything you like – perhaps a smoothie, guilt-free television, or spending some time with a friend.

The most important thing is to set up clear cues, routines, and rewards. Determine what your *"Craving"* is and be sure it is strong enough to make you do the routine/behavior. By taking the time to do this pre-work, you will set yourself up for success instead of failure.

The main purpose of habits is to solve the problems of life with as little energy as possible. Once we have habits established, we no longer have to think about doing those activities as they become automatic.

We'll talk more about creating your custom ***Spandex Habits*** plan soon. Next up, we will discuss why we procrastinate and don't follow through with something we really want.

Chapter 3 – Pesky Procrastination

Timothy A. Pychyl, Ph.D., a faculty member in the Department of Psychology at Carleton University (Ottawa, Canada), and his students devote their attention to understanding why and how we can sabotage our best intentions with needless delay.

In an article written on **Psychology Today**, Timothy talks about research they conducted on the connection between our emotional intelligence (EI) and procrastination, and they found a strong negative relation between EI and procrastination. Higher emotional intelligence scores predicted lower procrastination.

Timothy says:

"I believe that procrastination, the needless and irrational delay of an intended action, is primarily a result of poor emotional regulation abilities."

In their book, *Procrastination: Why You Do It, What to Do About it Now*, authors Jane B. Burka, Ph.D., and Lenora M. Yuen, Ph.D., explain the underlying cause of why we procrastinate:

"The emotional roots of procrastination involve inner feelings, fears, hopes, memories, dreams, doubts and pressures. But many procrastinators don't recognize all that's going on under the surface because they use procrastination to avoid uncomfortable feelings. Underneath the disorganization and delay, most procrastinators are afraid they are unacceptable in some basic way. As painful as it is to judge yourself for your procrastination, self-criticism may be

easier to tolerate than the feelings of vulnerability and exposure that come with trying your best and then landing in the territory of your fears. We know this is uncomfortable territory, but when you avoid your feelings, you are always unbalanced, picking your way through a field of buried emotional land mines, fearful about when you will stumble into the next explosion."

For many years, I believed I procrastinated because I had poor time management skills. However, after reading many books and looking at the research, I've realized that the reason is a lot deeper than "time management" or "productivity hacks;" I procrastinate because of my emotions.

If it were simply a matter of learning time management skills, we could all easily be taught those skills, and we would never procrastinate again. However, since it's more of an emotional issue and/or protection response, learning all the time management hacks and tricks won't fix why you procrastinate.

According to Burka and Yuen's, the Procrastinator's Code is: "I must be perfect. Everything I do should go easily and without effort."

The bottom line is that it's safer to do NOTHING than take a risk and fail.

For example, author Joseph Epstein says, "81% of Americans feel that they have a book in them – and they should write it." However, most people never write that book to avoid opening themselves up to criticism and analysis.

Procrastinators also believe that if it's not done right, it isn't worth doing at all. They must avoid being challenged because if they achieve success, someone will get hurt. Or, they erroneously believe, "If I do well this time, I must always do well."

A deep need for approval and acceptance influences much of our human behavior. It's encoded in our DNA and our brains. Doing things (like writing a book) and showing people your true self, exposes you to the risk of others not liking you or your work. Doing that can invoke intense fears and bring up emotional issues that have been buried for a long time.

Avoidance is one of the top defenses procrastinators use, and which prevents them from achieving their goals.

I know a lot about procrastination because I have struggled with this issue for years. I worked on my time management skills, my productivity skills, and my self-esteem. The emotional work I did had the biggest impact because it helped me understand who I am, my defenses (why I do what I do), and helped me become more aware of when I was self-sabotaging and procrastinating.

Years ago, a coach told me I was a high-functioning procrastinator. Sounds like an oxymoron, right?

She explained that I was not living up to my true potential, and although I was doing more than many others around me, I was living far below my abilities. She observed that I took some risks, but because I had deep emotional issues like "fear of success," "the disease to please," "perfectionism," and "fear of being seen," I was not putting myself out there.

I didn't think of myself as a perfectionist, but as I learned from Burka and Yuen's book, *Procrastination*, there are two kinds of perfectionists: adaptive and maladaptive.

Adaptive perfectionists have high standards and believe that their performance lives up to them. Maladaptive perfectionists have high standards, are excessively concerned about making mistakes, and are consistently disappointed in themselves because they don't live up to their preconceived standards.

It turns out I am a "maladaptive perfectionist," which explains a lot of my behaviors, such as procrastinating and not living up to my potential.

Perfectionism is an enormous block to achieving our goals and dreams. The perfectionist procrastinator expects more of themselves than is realistic – like getting in top physical shape in two weeks or expecting the first draft of their novel to be publishable quality worthy of a million-dollar advance. So, instead of motivating them toward accomplishing their goals, these high standards hinder their efforts.

Burka and Yuen explain more here:

"An important question to ask yourself is: Are you setting standards for yourself that enable you to make progress, or do your standards lead you to become discouraged, frustrated, and stuck? Your high standards don't make you a maladaptive perfectionist; it's how far below your standards you perceive your performance to be, how unrealistic and inhibiting your standards are for you, and how harshly you judge yourself for not meeting them. When perfectionism becomes a problem, procrastination is likely to become a problem."

In what areas of your life are you procrastinating? Do you have perfectionist beliefs like:

- **Mediocrity breeds contempt**. Everything you do must be outstanding, and if it's not, then it's mediocre. You devalue the ordinary and the average with contempt. You avoid mistakes.

- **Excellence without effort**. A mistaken belief that if one is truly outstanding, difficult things should be easy. Decisions should be easy! Writing a book should be easy! Picking a life partner should be easy! Instead of working hard and making an effort to achieve something, it's easier to avoid it by delaying it.

- **Going it alone**. Perfectionists are like lone wolves who believe they should do everything by themselves. They can't admit when they need help or don't have the answer. If the challenge is too much for them, procrastination is the answer.

- **There is a right way**. *My way or the highway* is the mantra here. There is one correct solution to a problem, and it is the mission of the perfectionist to find it. In fact, they won't take any action or commit themselves to anything until they find it. Rather than risk making the wrong choice, they do NOTHING. There is an underlying feeling that if they make the wrong decision, the feeling of regret will be intolerable. They live in a fantasy that they are omniscient and know and control everything.

- **I can't stand to lose**. Many procrastinators are extremely competitive, but they hate losing so much they avoid any activities that would bring them into competition with others. Competition is dangerous to a perfectionist. If you never enter the race, you can't lose, right?

- **All or Nothing**. If you have an all or nothing mindset, then you have a hard time appreciating any progress you make towards a goal. Like "mini goals," which actually do move you closer to your goals, but at a slower pace. You believe in going full speed and giving it your all, but you cannot maintain that pace, so you give up. One perfectionist said it like this, "It's either gold or it's garbage." Having this all or nothing mentality causes perfectionists to set big, unrealistic goals. When they don't achieve them, they feel like a failure. If the goal was to work out seven days a week, and they only made it to the gym three days that week, they feel as if they accomplished NOTHING.

I've always loved this quote by Theodore Roosevelt:

"It is not the critic who counts; not the man who points out how the strong man stumbles, or where the doer of deeds could have done them better. The credit belongs to the man who is actually in the arena, whose face is marred by dust and sweat and blood; who strives valiantly; who errs, who comes short again and again, because there is no effort without error and shortcoming; but who does actually strive to do the deeds; who knows great enthusiasms, the great devotions; who spends himself in a worthy cause; who at the best knows in the end the triumph of high achievement, and who at the worst, if he fails, at least fails while daring greatly, so that his place shall never be with those cold and timid souls who neither know victory nor defeat."

If we don't play the game, get in the race and into the *arena*, we don't have to take risks that might result in failure. This is the heart of being a perfectionist, and that is why procrastination is a symptom and not the cause.

We are all susceptible to living a life based on others' expectations, which are often unrealistic and cause us to procrastinate because we feel like we're not living up to everyone's expectations.

Accepting our weaknesses, our strengths, and liking ourselves is how we combat procrastination.

Remember, we are all combatting this internal voice that says, "It is safer to do nothing than to take a risk and fail."

Spandex Habits involves taking small, consistent actions and knowing that they will bring the results we want over time. We must understand our limitations and adapt our habits to our ever-changing lives.

We have to be vigilant about our tendency to procrastinate as we are building these new habits.

Do any of these sound familiar?

- I'll start early this time.
- I need to start this _____ soon.
- What if I don't start?
- I'll do it tomorrow.
- I should have started sooner.
- I'm doing everything, but…
- I hope no one finds out.
- I can't enjoy anything…
- There's still time.
- There's something wrong with me.

When you hear yourself saying any of these statements, realize that it's your *Inner Procrastinator*. Now you have a new way to combat that voice that says *do it tomorrow*.

Instead, you can say, "I don't need to do it tomorrow. If I do one mini habit right now, that will move me closer to my goals."

We all have days where we get a lot done and days where we procrastinate. I find that when I read books about procrastination, goal-setting, or time management, I am aware of my issues and consequently don't fall as easily into the habit of procrastination.

For example, I recently read a book by an author who makes a full-time living as a writer. He said that if he did not write first thing in the morning when he woke up – before turning on his computer, reading emails, making phone calls, etc. – then life took over, and he never got his writing done.

As soon as I read that, I knew I should start working on this chapter because the day would get busy quickly, and I wouldn't achieve my daily writing goal. My son and his wife had a baby a few days ago, and they are coming over for a visit. My daughter and three-year-old granddaughter are living with me, and they will wake up soon, and my granddaughter will say, "Glamma let's play." Then, I will have to choose between writing my book and playing with my granddaughter – and the guilt will kick in.

I can avoid all that by taking action now. If I have the energy or the time for a mini goal, that's good enough, and it will result in progress if done consistently!

We are not victims of our lives or those around us. We have choices.

I have a choice to wake up early and get my writing done every day or "procrastinate" and not achieve my goals.

In his New York Times bestselling book, *Essentialism: The Disciplined Pursuit of Less*, author Greg McKeown says:

"The way of the Essentialist is the path to being in control of our own choices. It is a path to new levels of success and meaning. It is the path on which we enjoy the journey, not just the destination."

I like what McKeown says about making tough decisions:

"In many cases, we can learn to make one-time decisions that make a thousand future decisions so we don't exhaust ourselves asking the same questions again and again."

In a way, this book is part of those tough decisions, but once we make these tough decisions about our goals and consequently our supporting habits, then those "one-time" decisions will make a thousand future decisions for us.

Don't underestimate the power of **Spandex Habits**. Having a systematic approach and clear goals will enable you to avoid decision fatigue or allowing others to choose for you.

When we surrender our ability to choose, we allow others to decide for us.

Choice is an Action

I live in a little cottage on the bay; when it comes to fixing things to maintain my house, I have perfected the art of "learned helplessness." I do not know how to fix basic things that most homeowners should know. I am at the mercy of other people when something simple breaks down. I now know that I am *choosing* to be helpless. When we forget we can choose, we learn to be helpless.

Don't ever forget or surrender your ability and right to choose.

It's easy to blame others:

- I have three kids to care for
- I have a demanding job
- I have a disability
- I have three jobs

- I don't have enough time in the day to do what I want to do because I'm busy taking care of everyone else.

I'm not attempting to diminish the real demands we all have in our lives, but I want you to see that you are not a victim; you have choices, and no one can take this power away from you.

You have the power to choose, and now that you have **Spandex Habits** as one of your tools, you have more choices and more freedom.

In the next chapter, we will explore the power of marginal gains…

Chapter 4 – Marginal Gains

We talked about all-or-nothing thinking in the last chapter. I've been an all-or-nothing person my entire life. It has worked for me (especially in business), but it's also worked against me.

You have probably heard, "Go big or go home." While I love the sentiment of that statement, it's not very practical or sustainable.

Ideally, I would like to be at my highest fitness level, with low body fat, strong muscles, and a lower weight. I used to think the only way to get there was to work out at the gym for 60-90 minutes every day.

Now that I'm older and life has become more complex, I can't devote that much time going to the gym every day; and the good news is I don't need to in order to achieve my goals.

I now have choices that can move me along the path to achieving my goals.

In his book, *The Slight Edge*, author Jeff Olson says:

"My observation is that about one person in twenty is achieving a significant measure of his or her goals in life; financial, professional, personal, marital, spiritual, in terms of health, in whatever terms you want to look at. Ninety-five percent are either failing or falling short."

One of the reasons so many people fail is because of the go-big-or-go-home mentality. It's not sustainable.

Most diets or fitness programs don't work because people stop doing them – not because the actions are wrong.

We don't do things that are hard for very long (unless we're training for a marathon or some other huge endeavor).

Olson goes on to say:

"Tapping into the Slight Edge means doing things that are easy. Simple little disciplines that, done consistently over time, will add up to the very biggest accomplishments."

Essentially, it's the little things you do every day (not the dramatic ones) that have the biggest impact and matter the most.

Whether you want to believe it or not – the *slight edge* is working in your life right now.

Invisible Results

When you make the right choice, unfortunately, you won't see the results immediately.

If I go for a three-mile walk today, I won't see results today – and that is actually a sign that I'm doing the right thing!

We live in a results-focused world where everyone wants to see results NOW. Fad diets that promise you'll lose 10 pounds in a week, but when you stop limiting the types of food you eat, you gain back 20 pounds.

Time either works for you or against you.

The secret of *time* is knowing that if you stay on the path long enough, you'll get the results you seek, and it won't be a question of motivation, mood, or attitude. You will know that time reveals everything.

A good friend of mine has diabetes, high cholesterol, and diverticulitis. He repeatedly proclaims,"Getting old sucks," as if *time* is the sole reason he has these ailments.

If we look at the previous five years of his life before he got these "lifestyle" diseases, we would see a diet high in sugar, processed foods, an abundance of fast food, and no exercise.

Time reveals everything.

People often don't change because they can't look far enough into the future to predict how their small, seemingly harmless "one" decision to eat a burger, fries, and milkshake today would affect their future.

Think about how farming works – *plant, cultivate, harvest.* – Our lives are the same. We are planting with our daily habits and routines, and then cultivating and harvesting the results over a long period of time.

It's easy to miss the repeated steps and choices that lead to remarkable results.

Here's a good example.

I love watching HGTV, especially the show, "Love it or List It." In each episode, we see the "before" house, and 60 minutes later, we get to see the "after" house revealed. However, we MISS the 6-12+ weeks it actually took to do the renovation.

Reality TV contributes to why we have a *disconnect from reality* – we see fast results that are unrealistic and do not see the whole picture.

The Water Hyacinth

Water hyacinths are beautiful and delicate with six petals usually in shades of blue, lavender, or pink. You can find these lovely plants floating on ponds in warmer climates.

The water hyacinth is one of the most productive plants on earth; one plant can produce as many as 5,000 seeds.

If the pond is quiet and undisturbed, the water hyacinth may cover the entire pond in 30 days. The interesting part is on the first day, you won't notice it. In fact, for the first few weeks you won't notice much. On day 15, you might see a single square foot of the pond's surface covered with the water hyacinth. On the 20th day, you would see a little bit more – maybe the size of a raft. On day 29, 50% of the pond's surface will be open water. However, on the 30th day, the entire pond will be covered by a blanket of water hyacinth. You won't see any water at all.

Daily habits work like this. We won't see visible results for a while, and suddenly, we will have remarkable results.

Remember this: The difference between success and failure is not dramatic.

In his book, *Atomic Habits*, author James Clear says:

"It is so easy to overestimate the importance of one defining moment and underestimate the value of making small improvements on a daily basis. Too often we convince ourselves that massive success requires massive action."

If we improve only 1%, it's barely noticeable, right? But if you can get 1% better every day for one year, you'll be 37 times better at the end of the year.

The opposite is true, as well. If you get 1% worse each day, you'll decline to almost zero.

Our small wins and small failures accumulate into much more.

Here's a great example of a marginal loss as explained by James Clear in his book, *Atomic Habits*:

"Imagine you are flying from Los Angeles to New York City. If a pilot leaving from LAX adjusts the heading just 3.5 degrees south, you will land in Washington, DC instead of New York. Such a small change is barely noticeable at takeoff. The nose of the airplane moves only a few feet, but when magnified across the entire United States, you end up hundreds of miles apart."

Time magnifies the margin between success and failure.

Your daily habits can either take you closer to your destination or further away from your destination. 1% better or 1% worse seems insignificant, but it has huge consequences and results over your life span.

How I Saved $100k In 12 Months Using Marginal Gains

I wrote a book detailing how I saved $100K in 12 months, Stop Living Paycheck to Paycheck, but I want to share with you a little bit about it here to highlight how marginal gains can build momentum and lead to huge results.

I earned six figures per year for many years but never saved a substantial amount of money. In March 2019, I decided that I was living on the financial edge, and not having money in savings wasn't very smart. So, I created a plan to save three months' living expenses by the summer – about $12,000. I hit that goal early, so I increased my goal to have six months' of living expenses in my savings account. Again, I achieved that goal quickly, so I increased it again to have 12 months' of living expenses in the bank. Rinse and Repeat. After one year, I had two years' of living expenses in the bank –$100k!

I didn't focus on or think much about having savings in my past. My goal was always to make more money – which, of course, is a great goal to have and achieve when you have your own business – but not saving for a rainy day is a mistake.

Like Warren Buffet says, "You only find out who is swimming naked when the tide goes out."

Weird analogy, but impactful.

I didn't want to be financially naked in a crisis.

It's amazing what you can achieve when you start small and remain consistent with your actions.

Next up are the building blocks for creating **Spandex Habits.**

Chapter 5 – The Building Blocks of *Spandex Habits*

This chapter will provide an overview of the building blocks for creating flexible ***Spandex Habits*** that fit your lifestyle.

Unlike our ancestors, we can automate habits using technology. For example, you can use an app to set daily reminders, track your savings and spending, track your daily steps, write books, and meditation.

We live in a time where apps and technology can work for you to transform complicated behaviors into easy, painless, and simple ones.

12 Apps to Help You Track Your New Habits:

1. Momentum Habits
2. Habitica
3. Productive Habit Tracker
4. StickK
5. Habitshare
6. MindSet
7. Streaks
8. Habit List
9. Balanced

10. Simple Habit Tracker

11. Habitbull

12. Strides Habit Tracker

You can find the links to each of these apps on lifehack's website at https://www.lifehack.org/668261/best-habit-tracking-apps

6 Apps That Can Help You Track Your New Habits/Behaviors:

1. **Save Money**: Mint, Digit, PocketGuard, Chime Banking, Simple, and Rize

2. **Sleep Better**: Headspace, Noisli, Pzizz, Slumber and Calm

3. **Meditate Regularly**: Chime, The Mindfulness App, Stop Breathe Think, and 10% Happier

4. **Lose Weight**: My fitness pal, Fooducate, Lose It, WW (Weight Watchers), and Noom

5. **Write Books**: Scrivener, Dragon Naturally Speaking, Write! Pro, Rev, Freedom, and Vellum, 750words.com

6. **Track Steps**: Pacer, Fitbit, GoogleFit, My fitness pal and Map My Walk

You can find an app for just about anything these days.

I'm sure you've heard the saying, "What doesn't get measured doesn't get done." We need to track and measure our goals so we know when we have achieved them.

Spandex Habits Building Blocks

- **Part 1:** Create mini, maxi, and massive sized habits that align with your goals.

- **Part 2:** Give yourself multiple ways to achieve each habit.

I recommend you track your habits with a Circular Habit Tracker template from Etsy (currently costs $3.44). You can purchase the template and print blank copies as needed.

If you would like to purchase this template, visit www.etsy.com/listing/750759706/bullet-journal-goal-planner-habit

My Habit Trackers

1. Fitness Habit Tracker – multiple ways to achieve your fitness goals, as well as mini, maxi, and massive levels.

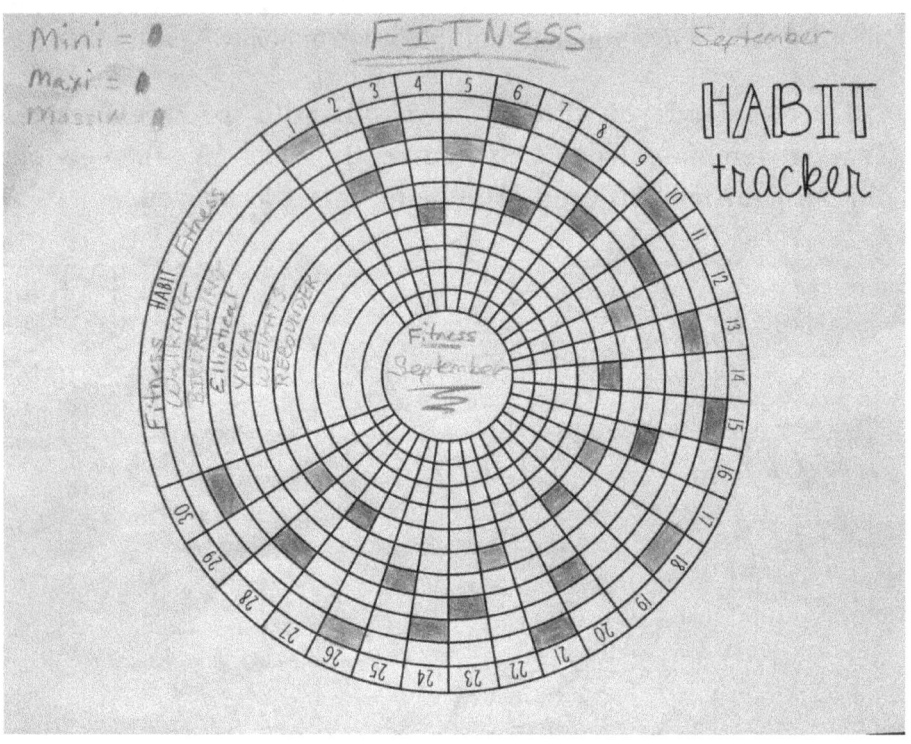

2. Writing a Book-A-Month Habit Tracker – multiple steps that need to be completed within 30 days (like writing my monthly book), as well as mini, maxi, and massive levels:

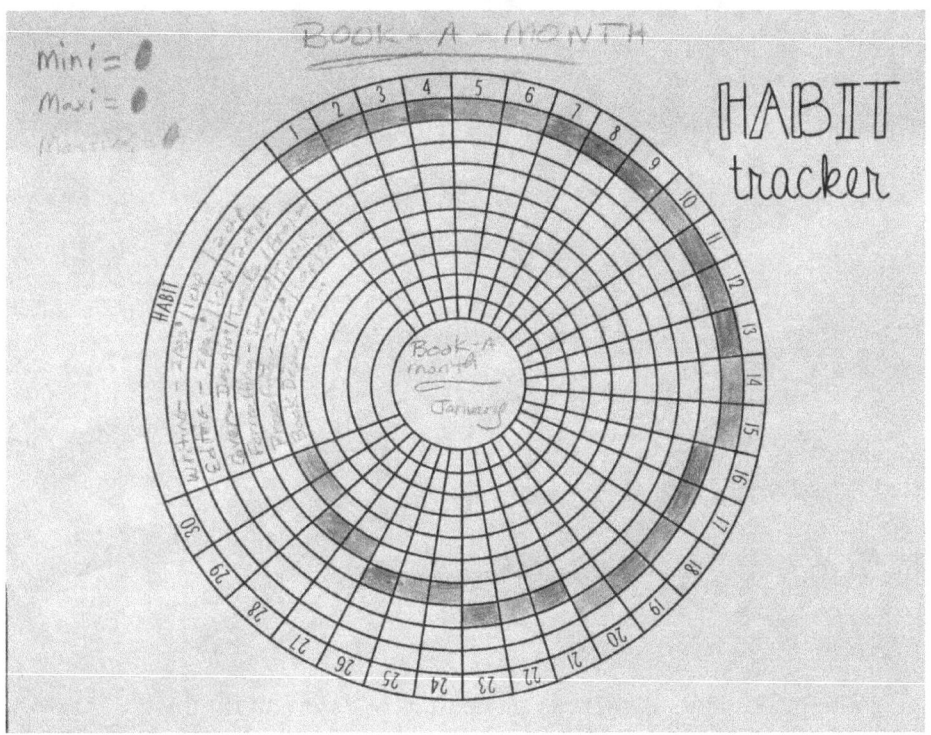

3. Morning Routine Habit Tracker – for routines you want to create or already established routines you have, with mini, maxi, and massive levels:

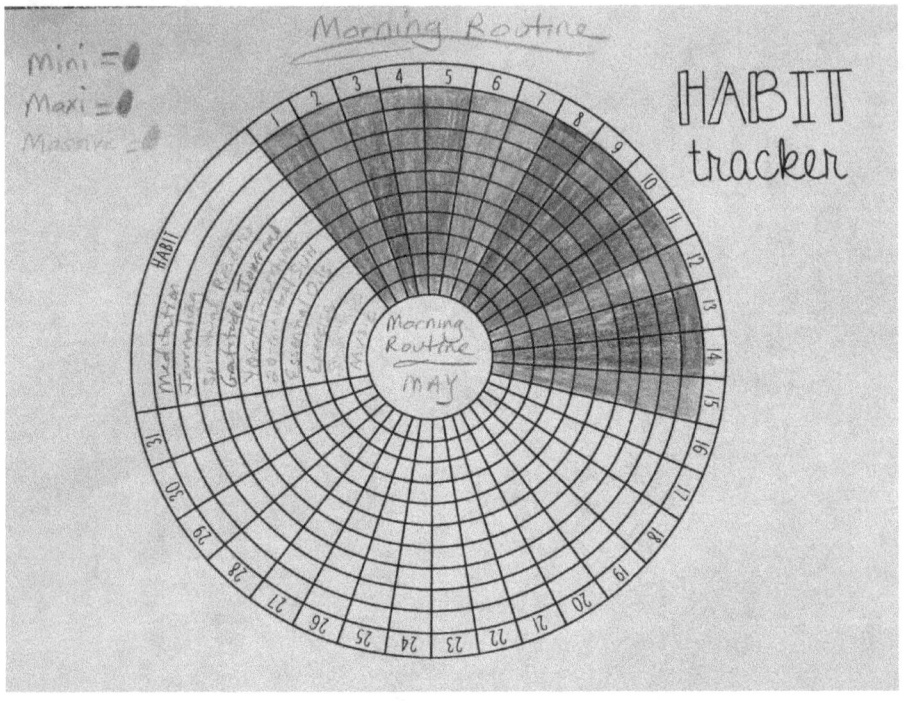

The good news is there is more than one way to do this.

If you like having routines, you could create one habit tracker sheet for each activity (fitness, finance, or cleaning). In an upcoming chapter, I'll talk about *Habit Stacking* to create routines around your habits.

Add More Activities

You can add as many "activities" to your chart as you like. On a tracker for cleaning habits, you could have a line for each room in your house; for exercise, you could include up to 10 different activities (Pilates, kickboxing, aerobics, etc.) on your custom habit tracker. Try to select things you enjoy doing. If you dread working out on a treadmill, then choose something you enjoy like walking around the neighborhood.

The sky is the limit now that you have multiple choices.

There is no right or wrong way to do this. The key is to find activities that bring you closer to your goals and create a variety of ways and time-frames or activity levels to achieve them.

Create Your New Habits Based on Different Elements such as:

- **Time** – a specific amount time (10, 20, or 30 minutes)
- **Window of time** – between noon and 4 p.m.; between 8 a.m. and 11 a.m., etc.
- **Action based** – ½-mile walk, 1-mile walk, 3-mile walk

If you make a chart for saving money, the choices could be to save $100 per month, $200 per month, or $300 per month. Alternatively, you could do a chart on percentages of income.

Rewards

Unfortunately, many people punish themselves if they don't achieve their ideal goals. So it may seem foreign to reward yourself after making small amounts of progress using mini habits.

Rewards are important to acknowledge your progress, action, and growth.

You can reward yourself after each activity, or after a certain time frame (weekly, monthly, or quarterly). On your Habit Tracker, write down what your rewards will be.

I recommend the reward be commensurate with the accomplishment. So if you achieve a Mini-Goal of walking around the block, don't give yourself a two-week vacation.

Rewards are best given immediately after the desired behavior because they work as *positive reinforcement* (like we saw with the killer whales at Sea World). To increase the likelihood you will repeat the action, make sure you have set up a reward system.

Here are some suggestions for rewards you could give yourself:

- Lunch or dinner at your favorite restaurant
- A smoothie or special treat
- A weekend trip to the beach
- Talking to a friend or relative
- Reading a book
- Watching a movie
- Self-Praise
- Taking a break
- Sitting in your hammock
- Doing a favorite hobby

For my fitness routine, I reward myself with a smoothie when I complete my mini habit. My reward for doing a maxi habit is a healthy meal out, and for three or more massive habits in a week, my reward is a new outfit or some exercise gear.

Decide what rewards you will give yourself, and be sure you follow through and give yourself the reward.

Jerry Seinfeld Never Missed a Day Writing Jokes

James Clear, author of *Atomic Habits,* wrote about this in a blog post: https://jamesclear.com/stop-procrastinating-seinfeld-strategy

Below is a quote from the post about the Seinfeld strategy:

"He said the way to be a better comic was to create better jokes and the way to create better jokes was to write every day.

He told me to get a big wall calendar that has a whole year on one page and hang it on a prominent wall. The next step was to get a big red magic marker. He said for each day that I do my task of writing, I get to put a big red X over that day.

After a few days you'll have a chain. Just keep at it and the chain will grow longer every day. You'll like seeing that chain, especially when you get a few weeks under your belt. Your only job is to not break the chain."

He goes on to talk about how mastery follows consistency.

All writers don't start out as "great" writers; the habit of writing creates better writers. You won't become a better writer by *thinking* about writing.

Jerry Seinfeld became a master comedian because he wrote jokes every day without missing a day.

That's why I love having a visual Habit Tracker. Of course, you can use a wall calendar, desk calendar, whiteboard, or whatever works for you.

In the final chapter of this book, you will create your own ***DAILY HABIT** planner*.

Next, we will talk about *Habit Stacking*, which is a great way to get more done in less time.

Chapter 6 – Habit Stacking

When we have habitual structures and routines in place, there is less likelihood we will get off track.

I don't know about you, but I can't remember what I had for lunch two days ago. Having a routine helps me remember what I want to be doing every day to achieve my goals. Left to my own devices, I'd go down a rabbit hole doing many other time-wasting activities, like scrolling endlessly on social media.

Established routines allow you to achieve what you want without requiring you to make decisions about it every day.

I didn't realize it at the time, but I was doing a form of *Habit Stacking* years ago when I created a "Morning Routine" checklist, which kept me focused and consistent. I created this routine because I realized I felt much better physically, emotionally, and spiritually when I did these things consistently. Here is what that original checklist looked like:

Morning Routine:

Date: _____

- ❏ Meditation
- ❏ Journaling (3 pages)
- ❏ Gratitude list

- ☐ Read one chapter in a spiritual book
- ☐ Yoga or Stretching
- ☐ Walk or Gym (3 days)
- ☐ Weights (3 days)
- ☐ Smoothie or Overnight Oats
- ☐ Take Vitamins

***Habit Stacking* is doing a string of behaviors in an organized sequence.**

I noticed that I craved the positive feelings I had when I did my morning ritual, and that motivated me to make this checklist and follow it.

Now that I have my *Spandex Habits,* I can add more choices to this list, such as a mini, maxi, or massive habit for each task and achieve a greater sense of accomplishment. Before *Spandex Habits,* I would regularly miss days of my routine when my life suddenly got busy.

Not everything on my Morning Routine list has a mini, maxi or massive habit associated with it because some of the items are one-time behaviors, such as taking vitamins or drinking a smoothie, but most of them can be Spandexed (I just made up that word).

Linking habits together allows you to get more done in less time and it helps automate your habits. Then, you'll have one string of habits you do instead of thinking about 3-10 different habits every day.

Examples of Habit Stacking Routines

Exercise

- Stretching
- Rebounder
- Jogging

Finances

- Balance Checkbook
- Transfer Money Into Savings Account
- Track goal in App

Cleaning

- Clean Bathroom Sink
- Clean Bathroom Toilet
- Clean Bathroom Floor

Organizing

- Declutter closet
- Organize closet
- Remove unwanted items from house

You can create routines for any of your habits. I promise you already do this naturally without even thinking about it. What is your morning routine right now? What is your evening routine? What is your cleaning routine?

We all have them.

For years, my evening routine looked like:

- ☐ Turn off television set 1-2 hours before bedtime
- ☐ Take out contacts and place them in cleaning solution
- ☐ Wash face
- ☐ Brush teeth
- ☐ Floss
- ☐ Turn on fan
- ☐ Read a chapter in a book
- ☐ Go to bed

The main reason we create habits is that our brain needs to conserve energy, and one of the ways it does that is through automatic habits. By "linking" habits, you are helping your brain even more.

In her bestselling book, *The Life-Changing Magic of Tidying Up*, author Marie Kondo talks about her routine when she comes home from work:

"This is the routine I follow every day when I return from work. First, I unlock the door and announce to my house, "I'm home!" Picking up the pair of shoes I wore yesterday and left out in the entranceway, I say, "Thank you very much for your hard work," and put them away in the shoe cupboard. Then I take off the shoes I wore today and place them neatly in the entranceway. Heading to the kitchen, I put the kettle on and go to my bedroom. There I lay my handbag gently on the soft sheepskin rug and take off my outdoor clothes. I put my

jacket and dress on a hanger, say, "Good job!" and hang them temporarily from the closet doorknob. I put my tights in a laundry basket that fits into the bottom right corner of my closet, open a drawer, select the clothes I feel like wearing inside, and get dressed, I greet the waist-high potted plant by the window and stroke its leaves.

My next task is to empty the contents of my handbag on the rug and put each item away in its place. First I remove all the receipts. Then I put my wallet in its designated box in a drawer under my bed with a word of gratitude. I place my train pass and my business card holder beside it. I put my wristwatch in a pink antique case in the same drawer and place my necklace and earrings on the accessory tray beside it. Before closing the drawer, I say, "Thanks for all you did for me today."

Next, I return to the entrance and put away the books and notebooks I carried around all day (I have converted a shelf of my shoe cupboard into a bookshelf). From the shelf below it I take out my "receipt pouch" and put my receipts in it. Then I put my digital camera that I use for work in the space beside it, which is reserved for electrical things. Papers that I've finished with go in the recycle bin beneath the kitchen range. In the kitchen, I make a pot of tea while checking the mail, disposing of the letters I've finished with.

I return to my bedroom, put my empty handbag in a bag, and put it on the top shelf of the closet saying, "You did well. Have a good rest." From the time I get in the door to the moment I close the closet, a total of only five minutes have passed. Now I can go back to the kitchen, pour myself a cup of tea, and relax."

I'm sure you are just as surprised as I was when you read that the routine Marie Kondo created took only five minutes! When I first read her routine, I thought to myself, "This lady is nuts; this sounds like it would take 30-60 minutes. Who has that kind of time?"

Now, we all can't be at the Marie Kondo level. After all, she is an organization Superstar who has sold millions of copies of her books and even has a television series.

The hardest part is creating the habit routine and putting it together in a way that makes sense for you.

Have you ever seen the movie *The Founder*?

It's one of my favorite movies ever! It's a story about Ray Kroc, who started as a milkshake mixer salesman and became a fast-food tycoon. Eventually, Ray convinced the owners of McDonald's, Mac and Dick McDonald, to allow him to franchise their McDonald's restaurant. Years, later he finessed himself into a position to pull the company from the brothers and create a billion-dollar empire.

Initially, the franchises weren't working because all of the franchisees were running their McDonald's venues differently and were not selling the same products. Ray knew he needed to create a *unified system* so that all McDonald's locations would look the same, feel the same, and sell the same items.

In the movie, *The Founder,* Ray goes so far as to orchestrate on a tennis court where the grill, milkshake machine, freezer, condiments, toaster, burger and fry station would be so that everything would work like a well-oiled machine.

It took some time for them to figure out where to place the equipment and how to organize everything, but once they did, it was truly magical! It looked like synchronized swimming. Every McDonald's franchisee now had to follow the new system, and each location was remodeled so they would all look the same. They even went on to create *Hamburger University* so all franchise owners would receive the same training.

It was a brilliant and strategic move by Ray Kroc that helped him become a billion-dollar success story!

Having "rituals" and "systems" will create more efficiency in your life and more success in achieving your goals and dreams.

In the final chapter, we will design your custom *Spandex Habits,* customized with habit stacking rituals to leverage your habits so you can be as efficient as possible.

Before we do that, we'll talk about how to reverse engineer bad habits that are holding you back from achieving your goals and dreams.

Chapter 7 – Reverse Engineering Bad Habits

When I worked in the legal field, I prepared cases for litigation by reverse-engineering the tasks that needed to be done in order to achieve the desired outcome (winning the case).

When I write books, I also reverse engineer the process. First, I look at the result I want to achieve, and then I work backwards. We can do the same thing with our bad habits.

In this chapter, we will reverse engineer our bad habits and then turn them into good habits.

My friend recently quit smoking and told me she gained 15 pounds. When she quit her bad habit (smoking), she replaced it with another bad habit (overeating) instead of a good habit (like chewing a piece of gum, or sucking on a mint, etc.)

If you quit a bad habit and don't replace it with something positive, you will probably default or slide into another bad habit. Eating isn't bad for you unless you're eating the wrong kind of food or large portions which will cause you to gain weight and can be harmful to your health. What we want to do instead is, replace the bad habit of smoking with something positive.

So let's reverse engineer a bad habit so you can see this in action.

In chapter 2, we spoke about the four steps to create a habit and how to break a bad habit. James Clear talks about these in his book, *Atomic Habits*:

How to *Create a Good Habit*

1. Cue – Make it obvious
2. Craving – Make it attractive
3. Response – Make it easy
4. Reward – Make it satisfying

How to *Break a Bad Habit*

1. Cue – Make it invisible
2. Craving – Make it unattractive
3. Response – Make it difficult
4. Reward – Make it unsatisfying"

Let's continue using smoking as an example of a bad habit we want to break since many people struggle with this one. I quit smoking more than 30 years ago, but I still remember how hard it was to do. And now, with all the addictive chemicals in cigarettes, it's not only mentally and emotionally difficult, it's also physically difficult.

When I smoked, my habit looked something like this:

1. **Cue**: I always had a pack of cigarettes in my purse or at the house.
2. **Craving**: I craved the nicotine along with the social aspect of smoking. I had anxiety, and smoking helped reduce my anxiety as well as my boredom.
3. **Behavior/Response**: Smoked a pack a day.
4. **Reward**: Removed my boredom and anxiety. Gave me something to do.

If I were to reverse engineer this bad habit so I could quit, I would do the following:

1. **Cue** – Make it invisible: Remove all cigarettes, lighters, and ashtrays from my home. Also, stop hanging out with (at least temporarily) other smokers.

2. **Craving** – Make it unattractive: Put large pictures of smokers' lungs all over my house to remind me of the consequences of smoking. I would also start working on my anxiety issues (meditation, therapy, reading books about it). I would find something else to do when I was bored; maybe read a book, listen to a podcast, call a friend.

3. **Behavior/Response** – Make it difficult: I would replace my smoking with a new habit such as chewing gum or eating mints or sucking on a lollipop – anything to address the oral fixation issue and give me something to do. I would not go to convenience stores or gas stations where I would see cigarettes and be tempted to get them.

4. **Reward** – Make it unsatisfying: I would give myself a reward for every seven days I went without smoking, such as a special meal out or a fun activity. To make it unsatisfying, I would watch videos of people who had health issues as a result of smoking to reinforce the future consequences.

Many bad habits have an emotional, spiritual, mental, and often physical element as to why we do them. Usually, these reasons fly under the radar, as we, unfortunately, have blinders on.

It's a good idea to analyze your bad habits to understand why you continue to do them. Of course, we're all different, so the reason I smoked might be completely different from the reason you smoke (or whatever bad habit you have).

According to researchers James Prochaska and his colleagues, there are four stages to how change occurs:

1. **Pre-contemplation** – When you're not ready to change and not even thinking about it.

2. **Contemplation** – When you start thinking about making a change and taking action.

3. **Preparation** – When you begin to take some action; you're not fully committed, but you're taking some baby steps.

4. **Action** – When you commit to the change and take action.

Michael Hargrove, a success coach and workshop leader, uses a similar 4-step model of change as follows:

1. Unconscious Incompetence (ignorance is bliss)

2. Conscious Incompetence (waking up)

3. Conscious Competence (choosing change)

4. Unconscious Competence (when actions become habits and we no longer have to think about them)

It's not as easy as the tagline "Just Do It." We actually won't do it until we get to the third stage!

Let's examine another bad habit that I struggled with for years – being in relationships with toxic men. Now, this is not your typical "bad habit" like smoking or overeating. However, choosing the wrong type of men became a bad habit because I did it repeatedly.

Right now, I consider myself a recovering jerk magnet, but it's taken a lot of therapy, emotional healing work, and several spiritual coaches to help get me to this place.

I lived in that *unconscious incompetence* state for many years – always wondering why I attracted these men and felt like a victim.

My last toxic relationship was with a very narcissistic man who had a lot of power in his career. We broke up 14 times over four years – it was like the movie *Groundhog Day*. I started reading books, listening to podcasts, and hiring professionals to help me break this bad habit. That was stage two for me – waking up (conscious incompetence).

After the 14th breakup, I was adamant that I wanted to change and decided I would do whatever it took to do so – that was the third stage – Choosing Change (conscious competence). I don't think I've arrived at Stage Four yet, where I have established an automatic habit of choosing healthy men, but I'm working on it.

I've done a great deal of emotional healing work, learned a lot about myself, and am much better at recognizing red flags that I would have ignored in the past – which was a big part of my problem. I also learned why I am attracted to these types of men, and am working on my issues so that the attraction is no longer there.

If I had to dissect how I broke this bad habit, I would say:

1. **Cue** – Make it invisible: I blocked his numbers, removed all reminders of him from my home, and stopped listening to songs that reminded me of him.

2. **Craving** – Make it unattractive: I still "craved" the connection with him long after the breakup, but when I felt that craving, I turned towards myself and took care of my own needs. I also wrote a list of the top 20 disrespectful and toxic behaviors he

had in the relationship, so I wouldn't have amnesia and go back to him. I had to constantly remind myself of his negative actions and not selectively choose to focus on his occasional good behaviors. I also had to stop living in fantasy land about him, wishing or believing things were different than they really were.

3. **Behavior/Response** – Make it difficult: I told everyone I knew that we broke up and I would never go back to that toxic relationship. I had an accountability friend so I wouldn't relapse. I also signed up for a year-long course on recovering from a narcissistic relationship, and purchased a narcissistic summit with talks from dozens of professionals, which helped keep me conscious and fully "awake" about my problem.

4. **Reward** – Make it unsatisfying: The reward was having no drama or trauma in my life. I made sure to write about this in my journal and on my gratitude list frequently.

Bad habits die hard. That is NOT an understatement.

Over the past 30 years, I've quit smoking, alcohol, sugar, and toxic men. By far, the hardest was toxic men. There were many layers of emotional issues that I had to address to break this bad habit. It took quite a bit of time because there were deep emotional wounds that had to heal, and it took years to work on those issues.

Breaking habits is not a one-and-done event; it's a process that happens over time, and you may relapse and backslide. Three steps forward and two steps back, as the saying goes. The important thing is to become aware, stay awake, and remain vigilant. If you have a bad day or relapse, you can practice "observation without condemnation."

Oprah Winfrey has struggled with her weight for years and is very open about it. She has repeatedly shared that she was an emotional eater. When she started keeping a food journal and writing down the emotions she felt when she would overeat or eat the wrong foods, that helped her make the connection.

Our bad habits feed something inside of us. Our job is to figure out what that is and work on that issue – whether it's mental, emotional, a physical craving, a spiritual matter, or all of these.

The longer we have bad habits, the more neural pathways we have created in our brains, so the harder the habits are to break.

"Neurons that fire together, wire together," according to psychologist Donald Heb.

The more you do something, whether it's good or bad for you, the more your brain responds to support that habit; it's actually trained to do what it is asked of faster and better.

This is why we get stuck in our bad habits and old patterns.

When I was a kid, my dad and uncles would take me, my brothers, and cousins tobogganing on the steep hills in Connecticut. Of course, the first time we went down the hill on the fresh snow, there were no established paths or routes.

The more we went down, the more tracks we created, and the deeper those tracks became. As the ruts got deeper and deeper, the faster the toboggan went.

In our brains, repetition lays down ruts or tracks, which is why we must be very intentional with our repetitious behavior.

Why Can't We Stop Repeating Bad Behaviors?

Pain is a great motivator – probably the greatest motivator of all.

I remember calling one of my friends when I had broken up with my ex for the tenth time. I felt as if I was going crazy and was powerless to the insanity. It was then I realized I needed outside professional help because I couldn't do it alone.

Einstein once said:

"We can't solve problems by using the same kind of thinking we used when we created them."

Sometimes we have to admit when we don't have the answers and acknowledge that we need to ask for help and support. To me, asking for help was admitting defeat or that something was wrong with me because I couldn't solve the problem on my own.

I know now that asking for help was a smart choice. Make sure you get professional help and don't rely just on "friends with advice."

A friend's advice can be helpful at times. For example, if you are trying to quit smoking and have a friend who previously quit, you can ask them for some tips on quitting.

However, some bad habits will require you to reach out for professional help. Just know that it's not a weakness to ask for help. It's what smart people do to get better and be better. We all want to have a good life. Bad habits can prevent us from living our best lives.

Addictions and Bad Habits Fill a Void

Finally, I want to talk about alcohol addiction because many people struggle with that as well.

I quit drinking in 1993 when I was 29; I had been drinking Jack Daniels since I was 13. Of course, there were many emotional reasons why I drank, and thank God I went to therapy to work on those issues. I also started going to Unity church and replacing my bad habits (partying, hanging out in bars, etc.) with good habits to fill the void.

Bad habits fill a void – spiritual, emotional, etc. Whatever it is, you must find a healthy way to replace that bad habit and fill the void in a positive way.

12-step groups and programs were created to help people eliminate their addictions by learning more about themselves, honoring their desire to become better, and live their best lives. They also fill a void.

I'll end this chapter by asking what bad habit are you committed to breaking?_____

To begin to eliminate this bad habit, I recommend you:

1. Read a book about the bad habit you want to break.

2. Listen to a podcast about this issue.

3. Find support for this issue.

4. Get professional help if needed.

5. Reverse engineer the bad habit to understand your personal cue, craving, behavior, and reward so you can break the bad habit.

I wish you much success in breaking your bad habits. Know it doesn't have to be a secret from everyone – we all have them!

Chapter 8 – Spandex Habits – Custom Planner

Now comes the FUN part! It's time to create your custom Habit Planner.

I recommend you start with 1-3 goals or one routine. Once you master that habit for 30 days, then add another. You can use the **Circular Habit Tracker** from Etsy, create your own, or use a planner, calendar, whiteboard, or whatever works for you.

Again, here is the link to purchase this template: www.etsy.com/listing/750759706/bullet-journal-goal-planner-habit

Or you can create a simple habit tracker like this on your computer:

Custom SPANDEX Habit Planner

Write your Mini, Maxi and Massive Habit in the Habit Column for each Habit
Example: Habit – Daily Walking – Mini: 1000 steps; Maxi: 5000 steps; Massive: 10,000 steps

HABIT	M	TU	W	TH	F	SA	SU	REWARD

HABIT	M	TU	W	TH	F	SA	SU	REWARD

HABIT	M	TU	W	TH	F	SA	SU	REWARD

HABIT	M	TU	W	TH	F	SA	SU	REWARD

HABIT	M	TU	W	TH	F	SA	SU	REWARD

HABIT	M	TU	W	TH	F	SA	SU	REWARD

HABIT	M	TU	W	TH	F	SA	SU	REWARD

HABIT	M	TU	W	TH	F	SA	SU	REWARD

Sample Goal Categories and Subcategories

- Fitness
- Healthy Eating
- Mindfulness/Stress Reduction
- Reading Books
- Writing
- Hobbies/Fun
- Career

- Romance/Intimacy
- Spirituality
- Money
    - Savings
    - Increasing Income
    - Eliminating Debt
- Self-Care
- Cleaning
- Decluttering
- Online Business
    - Social Media Posting
    - Facebook Lives
    - Creating Courses
    - Blogging
- Mental/Emotional Health

Review the "Clarity Questions" you answered in Chapter 1, particularly the following:

- What have I been struggling with for months or years?
- How is my life out of balance?
- What has my inner voice been saying to me that I have been ignoring?

- If I had a magic wand, I would change these 3 things in my life right now.

- What do I hate in my life right now?

When something is lacking in our lives, often it is a sign that we need to focus more on that area. If you've been taking care of everyone else for a long time and neglecting yourself, you could start with self-care and create a daily self-care routine.

In his book, *The Miracle Morning*, Hal Elrod, says:

> *"Every day you and I wake up, we face the same universal challenge to overcome mediocrity and live to our full potential. It's the greatest challenge in human history – to rise above our excuses, do what's right, give our best and create the Level 10 life we truly want – the one with no limits, the one so few people ever get to live."*

Spandex Habits will help you create a Level 10 Life!

Of course, when you implement a new habit, the first week or two is difficult, but it does get easier over time. The key is to be comfortable with being uncomfortable and remind yourself that this feeling of discomfort is temporary.

Neale Donald Walsh reminds us that, *"Life begins at the end of your comfort zone."*

In his book, *The Miracle Morning*, Hal Elrod provides readers a list of activities they can select from to start each day in a positive way. Some of the activities he recommends are listed below:

- Meditation

- Prayer

- Reflection
- Deep Breathing
- Gratitude
- Affirmations
- Visualization
- Exercise
- Reading
- Journaling
- Healthy Eating

Having a morning routine is a great way to begin the day.

People often tell Hal they don't have time to do a morning routine, so he developed "The 6-minute Miracle Morning."

Six minutes is better than ZERO minutes, and it can transform your life.

Print out your own Habit Tracker, use your planner, or write your habits in a calendar.

ACTION: Create your first Habit Tracker with either one goal or one routine starting now.

My first habit OR routine will be:

_____

Next, give yourself a few choices on how to achieve this new habit. So if it's fitness, give yourself 3-10 ways to achieve that goal such as: biking, walking, yoga, elliptical, etc.

For each one, add the details of the mini, maxi and massive version for each habit/behavior.

My first habit OR routine will be:

_____

My mini, max and massive habits for each routine are

Mini: _____

Maxi: _____

Massive: _____

Don't forget to reward yourself. If you're using the Habit Tracker, write what your reward will be for each mini, maxi, and massive habit you complete on your tracker.

That's it!

Here are the examples of how to use *Spandex Habits* with the Circular Habit Tracker:

1. Fitness Habit Tracker – multiple ways to achieve your fitness goals, as well as mini, maxi, and massive levels:

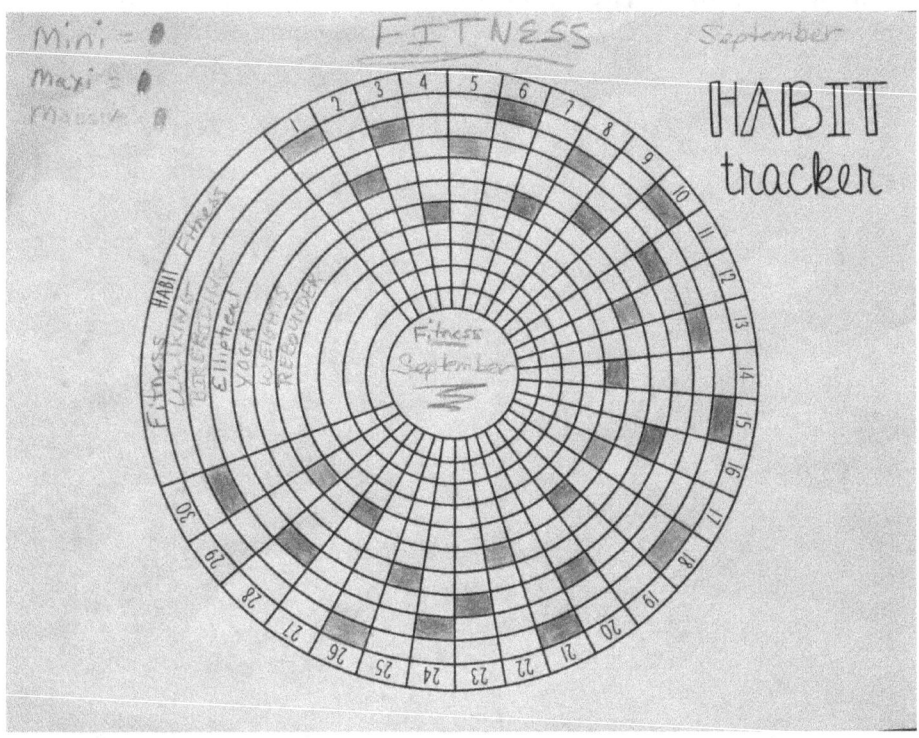

2. Writing a Book-A-Month Habit Tracker – includes multiple tasks to be completed within 30 days to finish my book, as well as mini, maxi, and massive habit levels:

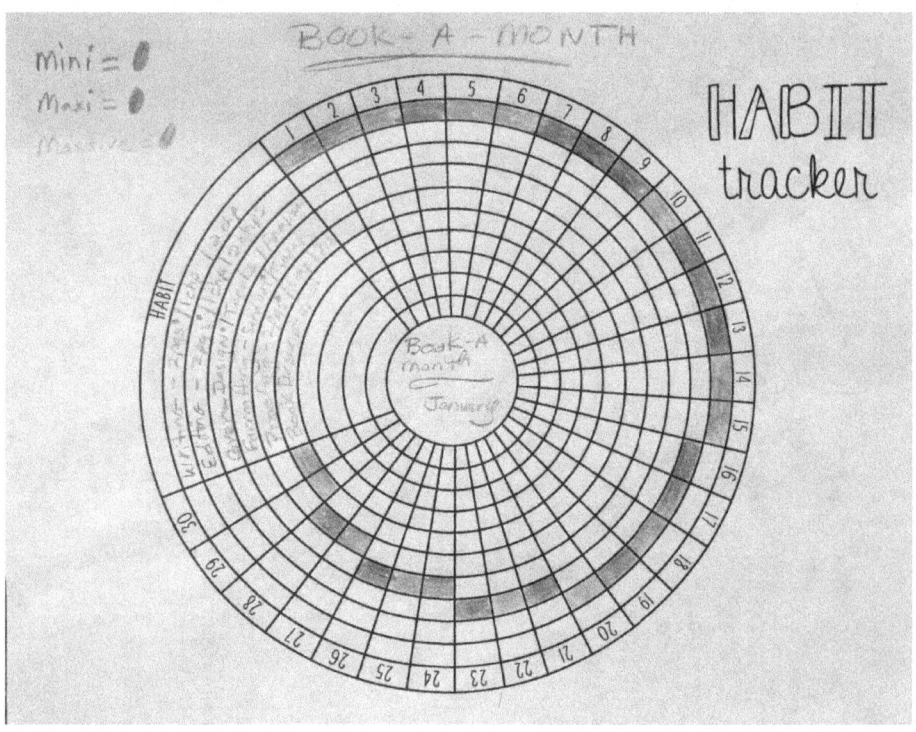

3. Morning Routine Habit Tracker – use for routines you want to create or previously established routines, with mini, maxi, and massive habit levels:

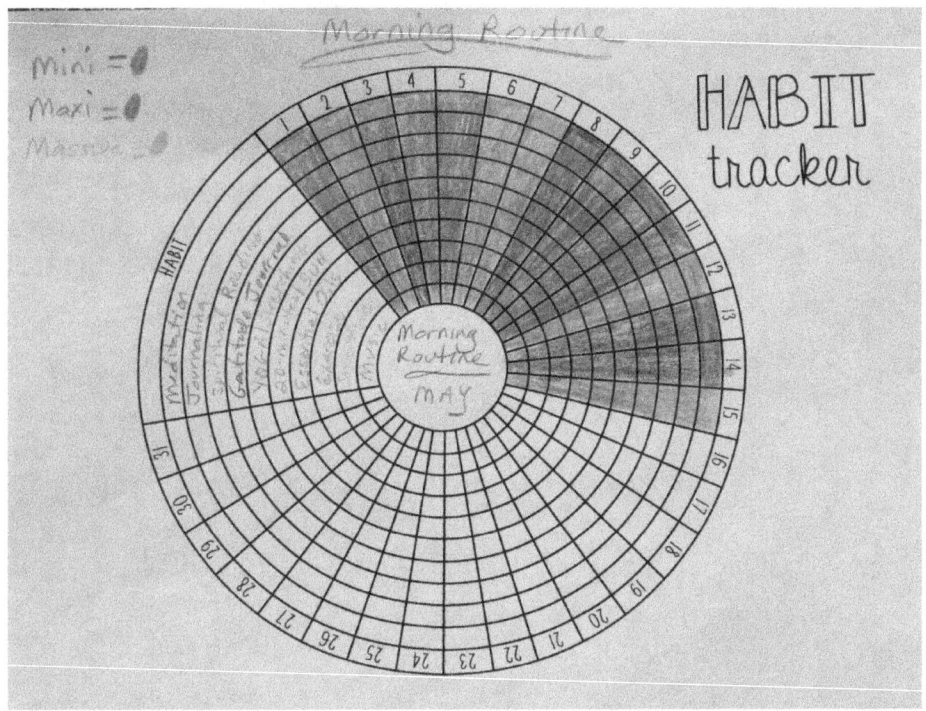

Make it fun and visual, and track it. Those are the keys to success!

Closing Thoughts

Don't wait to be great! Don't procrastinate.

You don't have to be perfect. You don't have to have BIG audacious goals. Well, actually you can have big audacious goals, but just break them down into mini, maxi, and massive habits.

If you do nothing but your mini-habits for the first 30 days, you are making marginal gains, training your brain, and creating a habit.

Many people are over-achievers or high-achievers. There is nothing wrong with having big goals, but if we don't have a flexible plan to achieve those goals, we will fail.

I never believed I could write a book a month until I made a public commitment to do that and created my *Spandex Habits* system to help me reach that goal. Because of my *Spandex Habits*, I have published eight books in 2020 so far; and by the end of the year I'll have written and published 12 new books.

I started at zero and am now am earning almost $2,000 per month in passive income from the royalties. It took me eight months to get to this point, and I'm glad I chose to use that time to achieve this massive goal – write a book a month.

I detail my book-a-month process in: 28 Books to $100K, if you're interested in learning more about writing a book a month.

I also have a FREE Facebook group you can join at: https://www.facebook.com/groups/28BooksTo100K

You can achieve massive goals and have remarkable results with this system. It really works.

Choices = Freedom.

I don't like having a tight schedule or strict routines, which is why I love *Spandex Habits*.

Because of this system, I feel good about myself everyday instead worrying about maintaining strict habits all the time or failing at my big goals.

I hope you will use *Spandex Habits* to achieve all of your goals and dreams!

Much love and success,

Michelle Kulp

Xxxxxooooo

Can You Do Me A Favor?

If you enjoyed this book or found it useful, I'd be very grateful if you'd post a short review on Amazon. Your support really does make a difference, and I read all the reviews personally to get your feedback and make this book even better.

Thanks again for your support!

www.ingramcontent.com/pod-product-compliance
Lightning Source LLC
LaVergne TN
LVHW051848080426
835512LV00018B/3132